Praying Through Lyme Disease
Book of Prayers

Rebecca VanDeMark

ISBN: 0692299343
ISBN-13: 978-0-692-29934-0

DEDICATION

To my mom, my best friend, who taught me the joy of praying through trials, and to my father, my hero, who has spent countless hours on his knees on my behalf.

CONTENTS

Chapter #	Title	Page #

Praying Through Lyme Disease

ACKNOWLEDGMENTS

All scripture in this book has been noted and there have
been numerous versions used to help encourage the reader
to look at a variety of different versions in their journey.
May you find rest, encouragement, and hope in the living
and active word of God and prayer.

AUTHORS NOTE

"Come and hear, all you who fear God, let me tell you what He has done for me. I cried out to Him with my mouth, His praise was on my tongue. If I had cherished sin in my heart, the Lord would not have listened' but God has surely heard my prayer. Praise be to God, who has not rejected my prayer or withheld his love from me!"
(Psalm 66:16-20)

At a recent Lyme Disease conference it was stated that "Lyme Disease is the growing epidemic and health crisis of the 21st century" and that "In the fullness of time the mainstream handling of Chronic Lyme Disease will be viewed as one of the most shameful episodes in the history of medicine". While not well known and maybe not well handled there are *hundreds of thousands* of Lyme Warriors that struggle each day just to live. Many of them cannot get out of bed due to extreme and debilitating fatigue and pain. Many are lying in hospital beds with doctors who don't know what to do. Many others are struggling emotionally under the weight of loss. Many others feel completely isolated and forsaken. In the midst of all of this there is a voice and a helper that calls through the dark night and says that He will never abandon or forsaken us. In the midst of sickness and pain it is hard to sometimes know how to pray through the scriptures of the Bible. This little book is designed with 31 topics that Lyme Disease patients struggle with and verses to meditate on and pray through in times of difficulty and in good days. This book is meant to be a companion and an encouragement to all who are struggling with Lyme Disease and the intensity in of their fight. Feel free to use this book in chapter order or simply use the chapters as needed. May you be blessed by the Lord. My prayer for each of you that pick up this book is from Psalm 20: 1-5:

"May the Lord answer you when you are in distress; may the name of the God of Jacob protect you. May He send you help from the sanctuary and grant you support from Zion. May He remember all of your sacrifices and accept your burnt offerings. May He give you the desire of your heart and make all of your plans succeed. May we shout for joy over your victory and lift up our banners in the name of our God. May the Lord grant *all* of your requests.

i

1 HOW TO USE THIS BOOK

Dear Fellow Lyme Warrior,

The book that you hold in your hand has been written from my heart. I found out I had Advanced Late Stage Lyme Disease the day after my 33rd birthday. For the previous six years prior to that day I had experienced a myriad of intricate and confusing health symptoms that never made sense to any doctor. I had spent hundreds of hours traveling across the United States talking and consulting with some of the best in the country. No answers came and I was eventually told that either (a) this was "in my head", (b) I had a very "complex case" of Chronic Fatigue Syndrome (for which I had been diagnosed for) or (c) "stress was contributing to these issues". Finally, after seeing 273 doctors in one year, seven years of searching, hundreds of invasive and painful tests, and thousands of prayers, I was correctly and accurately diagnosed with Advanced Late Stage Lyme Disease. While my family and I rejoiced that there was finally an answer, I also experienced a range of emotions as I was furious with the medical community and overwhelmed with where to go from that point on.

During this time and since then here are so many times where it is hard to know what to pray except for "please Lord, heal me" and yet (as with everything with Lyme Disease) I have found that there are so many emotions and issues that accompany Lyme Disease beyond that simple cry of my heart. Out of this journey has come the book that you are reading. My prayer with this book is that it will encourage you, lead you to scripture, and remind you that you are not alone in this fight. The journey is long and yet the Lord is near. I pray that this book is a jump start for your prayer life through this disease. There are 31 topics covered in this book to match the days of the months of the year. Feel free to go in order or to skip around to what is most on your heart. The word of God is living and active and I pray that you find scriptures that you can pray through that speak to your specific hearts needs. With each topic there is also a section of "prayer notes" where you can record your own prayers and scriptures and where you can visibly see how the Lord is answering the prayers of your heart day after day and month after month.

May the Lord bless you abundantly dear friend and give you strength for the journey before you.

With Love,
Rebecca

1

Rebecca VanDeMark

Praying Through Lyme Disease

2 THE DIAGNOSIS

"Yea, though I walk through the valley of the shadow of death, I will fear no evil; for You are with me; Your rod and Your staff, they comfort me."
-Psalm 23:4-

Lord, the news of this diagnosis of Lyme Disease has overwhelmed my heart. I know that "yea, though I walk through the valley of the shadow of death, I will fear no evil; for You are with me; Your rod and Your staff, they comfort me." (Psalm 23:4) I feel that I am walking in the shadow of the death because this diagnosis overwhelms me. I am so grateful to know the answer to the scary symptoms that I have been experiencing, but please Lord comfort my shaky heart. Scripture promises that "the Lord will go before me and that the God of Israel is my rear guard" (Isaiah 52:12). I am not alone in this fight Lord and while I feel that everything around me is shaken I know that your covenant of peace is with me. Even in the news of this diagnosis I trust you Lord. I trust the truth of Isaiah 54:10: "Though the mountains be shaken and the hills be removed, yet my unfailing love for you will not be shaken nor my covenant of peace be removed. Says the Lord, who has compassion on you." Amen.

PRAYER NOTES

_____
_____
_____
_____
_____
_____
_____
_____
_____
_____
_____
_____
_____
_____
_____
_____
_____
_____
_____
_____
_____
_____
_____
_____
_____
_____

3 CONFUSION OVER TREATMENT OPTIONS

"Think over what I say, for the Lord will give you
understanding in everything."
-2 Timothy 2:7-

Lord, one of the hardest parts of this journey is knowing
which treatment plan is the best for my body. So many
doctors, friends, family members, and others have so many
thoughts on what to do but I am confused Lord. Scripture
states that "you are not a God of confusion but of peace"
(I Corinthians 14:33) and I need that peace Lord. I trust
Lord that even though "we are afflicted in every way, we
are not crushed, we are perplexed but we are not driven to
despair" (2 Corinthians 4:8) because you God lead us each
step that we take. I trust that the treatment direction that I
take will only help me heal and beat Lyme Disease. I trust
that it will not harm me but only benefit me because Jesus
says, "nothing shall by any means hurt you" (Luke 10:19).
At the end of the day Lord I move forward knowing that
"you will give understanding in everything" (2 Timothy
2:7). Amen.

PRAYER NOTES

4 WISDOM FOR DOCTORS

"If any person lacks wisdom let him ask of God, who
gives generously…."
-James1:5-

Lord, I pray for every doctor and physician that I see that
you would give them wisdom in how to best help my case.
You say in your word that "if any person lacks wisdom, let
him ask of God, who gives generously and without
reproach and it will be given to him" (James 1:5). I pray
Lord that you would give wisdom and direct my steps as I
move forward (Proverbs 3:5-7). For every "medical team
member" that I see I pray you would give them specific
understanding about my case and understanding about
how to best help me heal. I pray Lord that "they would be
filled with all knowledge" (Colossians 1:9). I pray that you
would bless them abundantly as they work hard to help me
during my time of suffering. "May they be blessed by the
Lord, the maker of Heaven and Earth" (Psalm 115:15).
Amen.

PRAYER NOTES

_____

_____

_____

_____

_____

_____

_____

_____

_____

_____

_____

_____

_____

_____

_____

_____

_____

_____

_____

_____

_____

_____

_____

_____

5 FEELING DISCOURAGED OVER MEDICAL CARE

"She had suffered much under many physicians, and had spent all that she had, and was no better but rather grew worse."
-Mark 5:26-

Sometimes Lord when I have to see "other" doctors or those in the medical profession who are not familiar with Lyme Disease I walk out of their office feeling extremely discouraged. I know that I need their expertise to help me with issues that have arisen (either due to complications from Lyme or just for health issues in general) but it can be discouraging to hear their uninformed criticism of how I am proceeding forward with my treatment of Lyme Disease. Their words often cut and are extremely discouraging in light of all that I am dealing with in my treatment. Just like the woman in the gospel of Mark I feel that I have suffered much under many physicians. "She had suffered much under many physicians, and had spent all that she had, and was no better but rather grew worse." (Mark 5:26) Lord, unlike king Asa in 2 Chronicles 16:12, I am seeking help from physicians but I am also seeking YOUR help Lord. Help me to remember that these doctors I see are only human Lord and while they might not understand Lyme Disease you do Lord. I don't need to be discouraged by their lack of knowledge because YOU are the all knowing God. Lead me to the medical practitioners who can help me in my healing journey Lord and help me to forget those who have spoken discouraging words over me. Help me not to be discouraged by any medical care but help me to rest in the truth that you are the great physician (John 5:1-9). Amen.

PRAYER NOTES

_____

_____

_____

_____

_____

_____

_____

_____

_____

_____

_____

_____

_____

_____

_____

_____

_____

_____

_____

_____

_____

_____

_____

_____

6 FEELING LIKE A BURDEN

"Since they could not get him to Jesus because of the crowd, they made an opening in the roof above Jesus by digging through it and then lowered the mat the man was lying on."
-Mark 2:4-

Lord, as I fight Lyme I often feel like a burden to those who love me and take care of me each day. During difficult health days it is hard to see the look of pity and sadness on my loved ones faces and hard not to be able to wipe the fatigue of this battle out of their eyes. I know that they love me Lord, but I often feel like a burden. I feel like a burden as I know that the fight of Lyme Disease is a drain on everyone- emotionally, physically, and financially. I see the exhaustion that helping me brings both emotionally and physically Lord and I see the quickly dwindling financial resources. I feel like the crowds of necessities for fighting this disease are pushing in around me Lord just like the sick man in the gospel of Mark. And just like the love of the friends of this sick man, my loved ones do everything they can to bring me to where you are. (Mark 2:4) Help me to remember Lord that I am not a burden and that you have promised to take care of me and my loved ones. "Give your burdens to the Lord, and he will take care of you. He will not permit the godly to slip and fall." (Psalm 55:22) Amen.

PRAYER NOTES

_____

_____

_____

_____

_____

_____

_____

_____

_____

_____

_____

_____

_____

_____

_____

_____

_____

_____

_____

_____

_____

_____

_____

_____

7 GUILT OVER HOW LITTLE I AM ABLE TO DO

"If one suffers as a Christian, let him not be ashamed, but under that name let him glorify God."
-I Peter 4:16

Lord, in this fast paced and driven world, I often struggle with guilt over needing to rest or stay in bed due to Lyme Disease. Sometimes Lord the biggest accomplishment that I feel I have had is the ability to sit up in bed for the day. Compared to things that I was able to do in the past and things I feel like I was able to accomplish for your glory this seems like a failure. I struggle as I hear of others who seem to be able to do so much for you because they are healthy Lord. I often take what others are able to do as the measurement for what I should be doing and this makes me feel guilty over how little I am able to do. But Lord I know that I am not to compare myself to another. You say in scripture to "pay careful attention to your own work, for then you will get satisfaction of a job well done, and you won't need to compare yourself to anyone else" (Galatians 6:4). Lord, when I stop comparing myself to others and my past, I am able to see clearly the race set before me. "Therefore, since we are surrounded by such a huge crowd of witnesses to the life of faith, let us strip off every weight that slows us down…and let us run with endurance the race God has set before us." (Hebrews 12:1) Help me to "run" this race Lord for your glory and for you alone. This isn't about *me* Lord, it is all about *you*. I don't need to feel guilt Lord because I am not ashamed as I glorify you in this path you have set before me. "If one suffers as a Christian, let him not be ashamed, but under the name let him glorify God." (I Peter 4:16) Amen.

PRAYER NOTES

_____

_____

_____

_____

_____

_____

_____

_____

_____

_____

_____

_____

_____

_____

_____

_____

_____

_____

_____

_____

_____

_____

_____

8 WEAKNESS

"…As thy days are, so shall thy strength be."
-Deuteronomy 33:25-

Lord, today I am feeling so weak that I don't think I can even lift my head. This weakness is so debilitating that it is impossible to function. You promise Lord that "as thy days are, so shall thy strength be" and I am clinging to that promise today. "It is you God who arms me with strength" (Psalm 18:32). It is you God that arms me with strength for this battle with Lyme Disease. (Psalm 18:39). It through you Lord alone that I know that I am not defeated by this weakness because you have given me today so you will give me the strength for it. Guard my mind and heart with this truth Lord so that I remember this today. Be my refuge from fear and discouragement about this weakness and be my strength for this day. (Psalm 46:1) I love you Lord, my strength. Amen.

PRAYER NOTES

9 HEALING

"Behold, I will bring to it health and healing, and I will
heal them and reveal to them abundance of prosperity and
security."
-Jeremiah 33:6-

Lord, as I cry out to you every day I beg you for healing
from Lyme Disease, all of its co-infections, all of its
complications, symptoms, and everything related to Lyme
Disease. You are the great healer Lord. God it is you "who
forgives all of your iniquities; who heals all your diseases"
(Psalm 103:3). Lord, Lyme disease has caused destruction
and havoc on my body and on my life but you can heal all
of it. "He sent his word and healed them, and delivered
them from their destructions." (Psalm 107:20) You, and
you alone can heal and restore my health just like I read
you did when you walked here on earth. "And Jesus went
about all Galilee, teaching in their synagogues, and
preaching the gospel of the kingdom, and healing all
manner of sickness and all manner of disease among the
people." (Matthew 4:23) I cling to the promise Lord that
you will restore my health to me and bring healing! "For I
will restore health to you, and I will heal you of your
wounds…" (Jeremiah 30:17) You are healing me even
today Lord and I know that you are bringing health and
healing to my body. "Behold, I will bring to it health and
healing, and I will heal them and reveal to them abundance
of prosperity and security." (Jeremiah 33:6) Amen.

PRAYER NOTES

_____

_____

_____

_____

_____

_____

_____

_____

_____

_____

_____

_____

_____

_____

_____

_____

_____

_____

_____

_____

_____

_____

_____

_____

10 PAIN

"…Heal me Lord for my bones are in deep agony."
-Psalm 6:2b-

Lord, I am faint from the pain that is deep within my body. It hurts Lord to even take a breath. I would cry but the pain is so great that I have no tears left. Only soul wrenching agony of pain. "Surely you are my help; you are the one who sustains me." (Psalm 54:4) Because you sustain me Lord I will cry out to you in my pain and beg you for relief. With each breath that I take I cry out for help saying, "Jesus, help me". "My body and mind might waste away (due to the pain of this disease), but you, God are the strength of my heart and my portion forever." (Psalm 73:26) In my pain today and in painful and painless days ahead, "it is good to be near you God. I have made you, the Sovereign Lord, my refuge." (Psalm 73:28) "You are my God, have mercy on me Lord, for I call to you all day long." (Psalm 86:2) Amen.

PRAYER NOTES

11 DISCOURAGEMENT

"…This is what the Lord says to you: do not be afraid or discouraged because of this vast army. For the battle is not yours, but God's."
-2 Chronicles 20:15b-

Lord, so often in this fight against Lyme Disease I find myself discouraged. I know that you say to be strong and courageous and to not be discouraged (Joshua 1:9) but I constantly am. Between the physical symptoms and the emotional toll that Lyme Disease takes on my body I find myself more discouraged then hopeful. Lord you promise that you will fight for me and that I only need to be still. (Exodus 14:14) You also promise that this battle that I face is not mine alone but yours. (2 Chronicles 20:15) Be with me Lord as I feel so discouraged each day. Give me the strength to rely on your promise that you are with me in each minute and each day. I can wake up with confidence each day that you with me. (2 Chronicles 20:17) You promise that my faith in your Lord will uphold me. (2 Chronicles 20:20) Give me peace for my discouragement Lord as I rest in the promise of your word. Amen.

PRAYER NOTES

_____
_____
_____
_____
_____
_____
_____
_____
_____
_____
_____
_____
_____
_____
_____
_____
_____
_____
_____
_____
_____
_____
_____
_____

12 ANGER

" 'In your anger do not sin'. Do not let the sun go down while you are still angry, and do not give the devil a foothold."
-Ephesians 4:26-

Lord, sometimes in this journey I feel nothing but absolute anger at what has happened to my body. I am angry at this disease, I am angry at how my life has been affected by this disease, and I am angry that I must walk this path set before me. And sometimes Lord, if I am brutally honest I am even angry with you that you have allowed this to happen. Lord, I don't want to be angry. I don't want to waste the precious energy that I have being angry at anything but especially not at you Lord. You may have allowed this but you are good Lord and I have no reason to be angry at you. For if I stay angry Lord I am only a fool. Scripture says, "a fool gives full vent to his anger, but a wise man keeps himself under control" (Proverbs 29:11). It also says, "Do not be quickly provoked in your spirit, for anger resides in the lap of fools" (Ecclesiastes 7:9). I don't want to be a fool Lord. Take my anger Lord and place it at the foot of where it belongs- the truth that this is my temporary home and that this is a sinful world. While bad things happen you are still God and I release the lie that I should find anger at you. Help me Lord to release this and to use that energy to fall more in love with you and who you are. Thank you for being a merciful and loving God who listens to all of my emotions and reminds me to not let the devil have a foothold by holding on to anger. (Ephesians 4:26) What an amazing God that you are that you care about all of me- including my hurts and anger and you lovingly carry me through this journey. (Psalm 68:19) Amen.

PRAYER NOTES

_____

_____

_____

_____

_____

_____

_____

_____

_____

_____

_____

_____

_____

_____

_____

_____

_____

_____

_____

_____

_____

_____

_____

13 FEAR

"For you did not receive a spirit that makes you a slave to fear…"
-Romans 8:15-

Lord, one of the things I struggle most with on this journey is the feelings of fear over my current conditions but also of what the future might bring. I know that you say in your word that I have not received a spirit that makes you a slave to fear (Romans 8:15) but I am often in terror of what may come. What if my symptoms grow worse? What if I never beat this disease and spend the rest of my life in bed? What if the pain never subsides? What if something happens to my caregiver? What if… what if… what if… plagues my mind. I cling to the verse that says, "But now, this is what the LORD says— he who created you, O Jacob, he who formed you, O Israel: "Fear not, for I have redeemed you; I have summoned you by name; you are mine. When you pass through the waters, I will be with you; and when you pass through the rivers, they will not sweep over you. When you walk through the fire, you will not be burned; the flames will not set you ablaze. For I am the LORD, your God, the Holy One of Israel, your Savior; ……. Do not be afraid, for I am with you;…… Forget the former things; do not dwell on the past. See, I am doing a new thing! Now it springs up; do you not perceive it? I am making a way in the desert and streams in the wasteland." (Isaiah 43:1-5, 18, 19) Please Lord relive my fears and help me know the truth of these verses deep within my soul. Let me be as strong as Joshua when he commanded those under him, "Do not be afraid, do not be discouraged. Be strong and courageous." (Joshua 10:25) I leave my fears in your hands Lord. You are with me. I have nothing to fear for today or for the future. Amen.

PRAYER NOTES

14 ENVY

"They have no struggles; their bodies are healthy and
strong."
-Psalm 73:4-

Lord, as I struggle to even sit up in bed or get out of
bed each day I envy those around me who do not have to
deal with any health issues. From my vantage point Lord it
seems that "they have no struggles and their bodies are
healthy and strong." (Psalm 73:4) As I watch people go
blithely on their way or listen to the complaints of those
with no health issues I envy the cavalier approach to their
health. I envy that they do not have to be constantly
watching their health. I envy that "they are free from
common human burdens" (Psalm 73:5). I envy "that they
are not plagued by human ills." (Psalm 73:5) But Lord
when I live in envy I miss the blessings that you have given
me. I am not just this disease and your blessings abound in
this life you have given me. "You, Lord, indeed will give
what is good" (Psalm 85:12). Help me to focus on this and
not be caught up in envy that will only lead to destruction.
I know the truth of Proverbs 14:30: "A peaceful heart
leads to a healthy body but envy is like cancer in the
bones." Amen.

PRAYER NOTES

_____

_____

_____

_____

_____

_____

_____

_____

_____

_____

_____

_____

_____

_____

_____

_____

_____

_____

_____

_____

_____

_____

_____

15 WORRY ABOUT FINANCES

"So don't worry about these things, saying, 'what will we eat? What will we drink? What will we wear? These things dominate the thoughts of unbelievers, but your heavenly Father already knows all your needs. Seek the Kingdom of God above all else, and live righteously, and he will give you everything you need."
-Matthew 6:31-33-

Lord, as I find great comfort in knowing that the topic of money is addressed over 2,000 times in the Bible and that while on earth you spoke about this topic more than any other. You understand the heart of us humans so well Lord. You understand that we worry about finances and I *do* worry about finances Lord. It is hard to explain Lord the deep fear that I will not be able to provide for my basic needs let alone the treatment that I need to have to get better. Lord, I know that "no one can serve two masters… I cannot serve both God and money." (Matthew 6:24) And when I am not fully trusting you to provide Lord then I am not serving you. You promise Lord that "you will never fail me and never abandon me" (Hebrews 13:5) and I trust that Lord. Lord help me to live in the truth of Matthew 6:31-33: "So don't worry about these things, saying, 'what will we eat? What will we drink? What will we wear? These things dominate the thoughts of unbelievers, but your heavenly Father already knows all your needs. Seek the Kingdom of God above all else, and live righteously, and he will give you everything you need."
Amen.

PRAYER NOTES

_____

_____

_____

_____

_____

_____

_____

_____

_____

_____

_____

_____

_____

_____

_____

_____

_____

_____

_____

_____

_____

_____

_____

_____

_____

_____

16 STRENGTH FOR TREATMENT

"The Lord thy God in the midst of thee is mighty, He will
save, He will rejoice over thee with joy…rest in His love,
He will joy over thee with singing."
-Zephaniah 3:17-

Lord, if I thought being "sick" before the official
diagnosis with Lyme was bad, I had no idea how difficult
the treatment would be. I find myself so sick that I can't
talk, my pain is excruciating, and I am afraid that I won't
make it through. I need you Lord more than I ever have
before. My prayer is that with each medication,
supplement, or treatment there would be no adverse
reactions Lord, only help. You Lord are here and I do
believe that you are might and that you will save.
(Zephaniah 3:17) Lord, you promise that "God is within
her, she will not fall, God will help her at break of day."
(Psalm 46:5) Lord, help me believe this and know that you
will give strength to endure and make it through treatment.
My hope rests solely in you Lord. "Yet this I call to mind
and therefore I have hope; Because of the Lord's great
love we are not consumed, for His compassions never fail.
They are new every morning; great is your faithfulness."
(Lamentations 3:21-24) You have never failed me Lord
and you are ever faithful. I will rest in your love. Amen.

PRAYER NOTES

_____
_____
_____
_____
_____
_____
_____
_____
_____
_____
_____
_____
_____
_____
_____
_____
_____
_____
_____
_____
_____
_____
_____
_____
_____

17 LONELINESS

"Turn to me and be gracious to me, for I am lonely and
afflicted.."
-Psalm 25:16-

Lord, sometimes it is not a big event that I am forced
to miss out on due to being sick that brings out the intense
feelings of loneliness as much as it is the day to day things
that remind me how alone I am. Whether it is because I
am stuck in bed all day or whether it is hearing about the
latest coffee date I had to miss out on, my heart is heavy
with loneliness. "Turn to me and be gracious to me, for I
am lonely and afflicted." (Psalm 25:16) You promise Lord
that "you set the lonely in families, and lead for the
prisoners with singing…" (Psalm 68:6) I am lonely Lord
and I long to be set in a family and lead the singing. Lord,
please heal my loneliness. Let my heart be found solely in
you because you know me Lord – you know all of me. "O
Lord, you have searched me and you know me. You know
when I sit and when I rise; You perceive my thoughts
from afar." (Psalm 139:1-2) And Lord, you don't just
know me. You have chosen me. "For you are a people
holy to the Lord your God. Out of all of the peoples on
the face of the earth, the Lord has chosen you to be His
treasured possession. (Deuteronomy 14:2) And because
you know me and have chosen me I am never truly alone
Lord. I rest in the truth of these promises. No matter my
feelings, I am never alone because you are with me. Amen.

PRAYER NOTES

_____
_____
_____
_____
_____
_____
_____
_____
_____
_____
_____
_____
_____
_____
_____
_____
_____
_____
_____
_____
_____
_____
_____
_____
_____

18 FEELING FORSAKEN

""My God, my God, why have you forsaken me? Far from
my deliverance are the words of my groaning."
-Psalm 22:1-

Lord, with everything that has happened in this illness
journey, I struggle to not feel forsaken by you. On the
most difficult days I cry out with the psalmist, "My God,
my God, why have you forsaken me? Far from my
deliverance, are the words of my groaning." (Psalm 22:1)
In grief I cry out, "The Lord has forsaken me, and the
Lord has forgotten me." (Isaiah 49:14) And as my grief
threatens to overwhelm me you quietly and lovingly
answer me Lord. You say to my hurting heart: "I have
chosen you and have not rejected you. So do not fear, for I
am with you; do not be dismayed, for I am your God. I
will strengthen you and help you; I will uphold you with
my righteous right hand." (Isaiah 41:9-10) You remind me
Lord that I am worth more than the sparrows that you
take care of. "Are not five sparrows sold for two pennies?
Yet not one of them is forgotten by God. Indeed, the very
hairs of your head are all numbered. Don't be afraid; you
are worth more than many sparrows." (Luke 12:6-7) You
have not forsaken me Lord, you are always with me. You
promise, "I will never leave you nor forsake you"
(Deuteronomy 31:6) and it is that truth I cling to. Amen.

PRAYER NOTES

_____

_____

_____

_____

_____

_____

_____

_____

_____

_____

_____

_____

_____

_____

_____

_____

_____

_____

_____

_____

_____

_____

_____

19 LOSS OF WHO I WAS

"How can we sing the songs of the Lord while in a foreign land?"
-Psalm 137:4-

Lord, the God who knows me even when I don't recognize myself or my life, I come to you knowing that *you* Lord are unchanging. You, precious Savior "are the same yesterday, today, and forever". (Hebrews 13:8) Remind me Lord when I feel dizzy with the changes that this disease has brought that *you* have not changed. Bring to mind the truth of scripture and who you are Lord. Help me to cling to the truth that there is *no* circumstance that is touching my life that you have not allowed or deemed best for me. When the waves of despair for all that this disease has taken sweep over me, guide me Lord into your truth. My heart cries out with the psalmist who wrote, "How can we sing the songs of the Lord while in a foreign land"? (Psalm 137:4). I feel that everyday I am walking in a foreign land Lord. My life might look vastly different then it was or what I planned for it to be but I rest in peace knowing that *you* Lord never change. "You are my refuge; my portion in the land of the living". (Psalm 141:5) Amen.

PRAYER NOTES

_____

_____

_____

_____

_____

_____

_____

_____

_____

_____

_____

_____

_____

_____

_____

_____

_____

_____

_____

_____

_____

_____

20 COMPARING THE PAST TO THE PRESENT

"Do not say 'why were the old days betters than these' for it is not wise to ask such questions."
-Ecclesiastes 7:10-

Lord, if there is one battle that I fight with my mind *all* of the time it is the temptation to allow the past to be better than today. It is so easy to compare life as of now to "BL" (Before Lyme). Lord you say in scripture that it is not wise to ask the questions of why the old days were better than these. (Ecclesiastes 7:10) To be honest Lord I am not sure why except for the fact that by living in those questions I miss the blessings of the present. You promise Lord that "I will see the good in the land of the living". (Psalm 27:13) Living is not in the past but in the present. Lord, you are the God of the past and I thank you for all of the wonderful memories and experiences that I had in the past. Even for the things that I didn't thank you for at the time but now recognize as joy. Thank you. Lord, I am content though with where you have me now. There is life after the diagnosis of Lyme Disease. Show me Lord the way to live so that I remain humbly grateful for the past but can view the present as the gift that it is. Amen.

PRAYER NOTES

_____
_____
_____
_____
_____
_____
_____
_____
_____
_____
_____
_____
_____
_____
_____
_____
_____
_____
_____
_____
_____
_____
_____
_____
_____

21 GRIEF OVER THE WAY I ENVISIONED LIFE TO BE LIKE

"I will repay you for the years the locusts have stolen…"
-Joel 2:28-

Lord, this is not how I envisioned my life, at my age to look like. In my wildest dreams this would have been farther then I could have ever imagined. I long for _____ and instead I am on my sickbed. I am in grief Lord, grief over the way I envisioned life to be like. I am grieving. Scripture promises that "God will never forget the needy; the hope of the afflicted will never perish". (Psalm 9:18) I am definitely needy Lord and I know that you have not forgotten me. Lord, while my days are not what I envisioned or dreamed right now, I know that you will repay the years that this disease has stolen from me. You promise that you "will repay (me) for the years that the locusts have stolen". (Joel 2:28) And I rest in this promise Lord and in the peace of knowing that while I might never have dreamt this for my life, "I trust in you Lord, I say, 'you are my God'. My times are in your hands". (Psalm 31:14-15) Amen.

PRAYER NOTES

22 GRIEF OVER LOSS OF FRIENDS

"Scorn has broken my heart and has left me helpless; I looked for sympathy, but there was none, for comforters, but I found none."
-Psalm 69:20-

Lord, you know the heartbreak that I am experiencing right now as I have lost friends. My heart is broken as I feel like I have experienced death ten times over as friends have walked away. Lord you know that, "scorn has broken my heart and has left me helpless; I looked for sympathy, but there was none, for comforters but I found none."(Psalm 69:20) Lord, mend my heart and heal it. "You are close to the brokenhearted Lord and you save those crushed in spirit" (Psalm 34:18) so I know that you will comfort me and save me. "You heal the brokenhearted and bind up their wounds" (Psalm 147:3). I cling to this promise Lord that you will heal this gaping wound in my heart. "Because you are my help, I will sing in the shadow of your wings" (Psalm 63:7) Amen.

PRAYER NOTES

_____

_____

_____

_____

_____

_____

_____

_____

_____

_____

_____

_____

_____

_____

_____

_____

_____

_____

_____

_____

_____

_____

_____

23 GRIEF OVER LOSS OF FAMILY

"…"Can a mother forget the baby at her breast and have no compassion on the child she has borne? Though she may forget, I will not forget you! See, I have engraved you on the palms of my hands…"
-Isaiah 49:15-16-

Lord, my grief is heavy as I am experiencing a pain so deep words can not even speak the depth of my loss. I have been left alone as the family member (or members) that I expected to walk with this journey with me are unable or unwilling to do so. "I have become estranged from my brothers and an alien to my mother's sons." (Psalm 68:9) Lord you promise that "you are close to the brokenhearted" (Psalm 34:18) and I am completely brokenhearted. This wound has pierced my heart and I beg you for healing Lord. Help me to remember that it is YOU lord, no one else that will walk this journey with me. "It is God who arms me with strength and makes my way perfect." (Psalm 18:32) No matter who leaves me on this journey Lord I am never alone because you are with me. "Though my father and mother forsake me, the Lord will receive me." (Psalm 27:10) You will never abandon me because you have engraved me on the palms of your hands! "Can a mother forget the baby at her breast and have no compassion on the child she has borne? Though she may forget, I will not forget you! See, I have engraved you on the palms of my hands…" (Isaiah 49:15-16) Amen.

PRAYER NOTES

_____

_____

_____

_____

_____

_____

_____

_____

_____

_____

_____

_____

_____

_____

_____

_____

_____

_____

_____

_____

_____

_____

_____

24 GRIEF OVER LACK OF UNDERSTANDING

"There is one whose rash words are like sword thrusts...."
-Proverbs 12:18-

Lord, you know the heartbreak when hasty words are spoken to me and show a lack of understanding of what I am dealing with in regards to this disease. Whether it is a well intentioned word or a purposeful hurtful word, the lack of understanding cuts to the heart. Truly Lord, "Death and life are in the power of the tongue..." (Proverbs 18:21) Words that are all too common that I and others hear speak "death" and not "life" to my situation. Help me to forgive those who have hurt me with their words Lord. Help me to remember that my own words have the power of life and death. Lord, teach me to not speak death over my situation or another's situation. Help me to only speak what "is good for building up, as fits the occasion" (Ephesians 4:29). You are the God of life and I pray that my heart would overflow and speak this truth. "May the words of my mouth and the meditation of my heart be pleasing to you, O Lord, my rock and my redeemer." (Psalm 19:14) Amen.

PRAYER NOTES

_____

_____

_____

_____

_____

_____

_____

_____

_____

_____

_____

_____

_____

_____

_____

_____

_____

_____

_____

_____

_____

25 FORGIVENESS

"And when you stand praying, if you hold anything against anyone, forgive them, so that your Father in heaven may forgive you your sins."
-Mark 11:25-

Lord, you state in scripture that we are to forgive others. You state in Ephesians that we should "get rid of all bitterness, rage and anger, brawling and slander, along with every form of malice and be kind and compassionate to one another, forgiving each other, just as in Christ God forgave you" (Ephesians 4:31-32) I know Lord that there are studies done that show links between health issues and un-forgiveness and I believe in your word you speak about forgiving others. We are to "forgive as you have forgiven us" (Colossians 3:13) I don't want to hold onto anything that might detriment my healing Lord including un-forgiveness. Please help me to forgive those who have hurt me (whether in the past or in the present) and help me to place them in your care Lord. Please forgive my own sins Lord that I commit. Thank you for your grace and forgiveness in my life Lord. It is amazing how you have forgiven me. Your love shouts of great love that I can share with others through forgiveness. Thank you Lord. Amen.

PRAYER NOTES

_____

_____

_____

_____

_____

_____

_____

_____

_____

_____

_____

_____

_____

_____

_____

_____

_____

_____

_____

_____

_____

_____

_____

_____

26 THE BATTLE THAT NEVER ENDS

"… the Lord has heard my weeping. The Lord has heard
my cry for mercy…"
-Psalm 6:8-9-

Have mercy on me Lord, for I am faint; heal me, Lord, for
my bones are in agony. (Psalm 6:2) This battle Lord seems
never-ending. Each night as I lay awake I weep with
longing to be healed. "I am worn out from groaning Lord.
All night long I flood my bed with weeping and drench my
couch with tears. My eyes grow weak with sorrow." (Psalm
6: 6-7) Like the psalmist Lord I look at this battle with this
awful disease and "my soul is filled with deep anguish.
How long Lord, how long" (Psalm 6:3) will this illness
last? Please Lord turn to me. Hear my cry and my
supplication. "Turn and deliver me; save me because of
your unfailing love." (Psalm 6:4) Thank you Lord that my
prayers for this battle that seems so long are not in vain.
Thank You, "Lord that you have heard my weeping.
Thank You, Lord that you have heard my cry for mercy
and that you accept my prayer." (Psalm 6:8-9) Amen.

PRAYER NOTES

_____

_____

_____

_____

_____

_____

_____

_____

_____

_____

_____

_____

_____

_____

_____

_____

_____

_____

_____

_____

_____

_____

_____

_____

27 HOPE

"O Israel, hope in the Lord; for with the Lord there is
unfailing love. His redemption overflows.."
-Psalm 130:7-

Lord, hope is a waning thing as the days grow long
with suffering. I find myself questioning what I hope in
and what my hope is placed on. If it is on healing Lord
that is not enough as my hope must be placed on YOU
completely and solely. Lord, "my soul waits for you. You
are my help and my shield…O Lord, be upon us, even as
we hope in you." (Psalm 33:30-22) As I put my hope in
you alone Lord I know that I will find unfailing love.
(Psalm 130:7) My hope is secure in you Lord and my hope
of a future is trustworthy because you promise that the
plans that you have for me are plans to give me a future
and hope. (Jeremiah 29:11) "So we do not lose heart
(Lord). Though our outer self is wasting away, our inner
self is being renewed day by day. For this light momentary
affliction is preparing for us an eternal weight of glory
beyond all comparison, as we look not to the things that
are seen but to the things that are unseen. For the things
that are seen are transient, but the things that are unseen
are eternal." (2 Corinthians 4:16-18) Amen.

PRAYER NOTES

_____

_____

_____

_____

_____

_____

_____

_____

_____

_____

_____

_____

_____

_____

_____

_____

_____

_____

_____

_____

_____

_____

_____

28 PURPOSE IN OUR PAIN

"Blessed be the God and Father of our Lord Jesus Christ, the Father of mercies and God of all comfort, who comforts us in all of our affliction, so that we may be able to comfort with which we ourselves are comforted by God."
-2 Corinthians 1:3-4-

Lord, in the midst of this battle with Lyme Disease I find myself at a loss of what my purpose could possibly be. I feel so week myself that the thought of finding a "great big purpose" is not overwhelming but seemingly impossible (especially on the days I can't do anything but lay in bed!). But Lord, I also look around and I see there are so many hurting people just like myself. I see the vast multitudes of the brokenhearted- not only physically but emotionally as well. You Lord are "the Father of mercies and God of all comfort, who comforts us in all of our affliction, so that we may be able to comfort with which we ourselves are comforted..." (2 Corinthians 1:3-4). Lord, YOU are the great comforter. Show me each day the purpose in my pain and this illness. Show me who I can comfort as you have comforted me. Show me needs your love Lord and how I can do it. Thank you Lord. Amen.

PRAYER NOTES

_____
_____
_____
_____
_____
_____
_____
_____
_____
_____
_____
_____
_____
_____
_____
_____
_____
_____
_____
_____
_____
_____
_____
_____

29 DESIRES OF MY HEART

"May He give you the desires of your heart and make all of
your plans succeed. May we shout for joy... May the Lord
grant all of your requests."
-Psalm 20:4-5-

Lord, it seems that on this journey I have had to give
up so many hopes, dreams, and desires for the future.
Specifically the immediate future. I see my dream of
_____ passing me by and it breaks my heart.
You promise Lord that if we "take delight in You, You will
give us the desires of our hearts". (Psalm 37:4) I want to
delight in You alone Lord but sometimes my desires and
dreams for my future seem to loom before me and take
my eyes off of you. Give me your heart Lord. Comfort me.
I pray that you would take my eyes off of the thing (or
things) that I think I am missing and put them back on you
completely. When I see others getting things that I wanted
help to me rejoice with them knowing that you are
working in both of our lives according to your perfect will.
(Romans 12:15) This is not about losing the desires of my
heart Lord, its about surrendering to your love and your
plans and I do that Lord with open hands. "For you Lord
are good and what you do is good." (Psalm 119:68) And
"the Lord is good and your love endures forever." (Psalm
100:5) You are good and I trust you completely. Amen.

PRAYER NOTES

_____

_____

_____

_____

_____

_____

_____

_____

_____

_____

_____

_____

_____

_____

_____

_____

_____

_____

_____

_____

_____

_____

_____

30 TAKING ONE DAY AT A TIME

"So don't be anxious about tomorrow. God will take care
of your tomorrow too. Live one day at a time."
-Matthew 6:34-

Lord, help me to remember that on this journey of life
all I need to do is take one day at a time. You say in
scripture, "don't be anxious about tomorrow. God will
take care of your tomorrow too. Live one day at a time"
(Matthew 6:34) and I want to do that Lord. Sometimes all
I can see is the pain, the difficulty of this disease, and all of
the symptoms that I am experiencing. It is hard to
remember that all we have is today. I put my hopes, my
concerns, and my fears in your hands Lord. "Cast your
cares on the Lord and He will sustain you; He will never
let the righteous be shaken." (Psalm 55:22) I am casting
my cares on you Lord. I know that you can handle all of
my fears for what tomorrow may bring. You promise to
cover us Lord and to be our shield. "He will cover you
with His feathers, and under His wings you will find
refuge; His faithfulness will be your shield and rampart."
(Psalm 91:4) All I have is today Lord the future is in your
hands. I have no fear because you promise that you are not
only hear today but with me tomorrow. "The Lord is
there…"(Ezekiel 48:35) Amen.

PRAYER NOTES

_____

_____

_____

_____

_____

_____

_____

_____

_____

_____

_____

_____

_____

_____

_____

_____

_____

_____

_____

_____

_____

_____

_____

_____

31 CHOOSING JOY

"Today I have given you the choice between life and death, between blessings and curses. Now I call on heaven and earth to witness the choice you make. Oh that you would choose life, so that you and your descendants might live."
-Deuteronomy 30:19-

Lord, today, despite all of the symptoms of Lyme Disease, all of the side effects of treatment, and all of the health issues I want to choose life. I want to choose joy. You say, "today I have given you the choice between life and death, between blessings and curses. Now I call on heaven and earth to witness the choice you make. Oh that you would choose life so that you and your descendants might live" (Deuteronomy 30:19) Lord I want to choose life in this situation even though I feel so terrible. I know that in choosing life I will be choosing joy. You say in scripture to "consider it pure joy… whenever you face trials of many kinds, because you know that the testing of your faith develops perseverance" (James 1:2-3) and Lord that perseverance is reminding me that all joy, no matter our circumstances is found only in you. Lord, "the hope of the righteous is joy" (Proverbs 10:28) and that is where I find my joy completely. In finding my hope in you. Help me Lord to choose joy today. Help me to choose finding joy and life in you. Amen.

PRAYER NOTES

_____
_____
_____
_____
_____
_____
_____
_____
_____
_____
_____
_____
_____
_____
_____
_____
_____
_____
_____
_____
_____
_____
_____
_____
_____

32 HOPE FOR THE FUTURE

"She is clothed with strength and dignity; she can laugh at
the days to come."
-Proverbs 31:25-

Lord, sometimes I look at my reflection in the mirror
and I don't know the person staring back at me. So much
has changed physically, emotionally, and mentally in this
journey. I sometimes long for life to be "normal" and yet I
have no idea what "normal" would look like anymore. Let
my fears, my hopes, my longings, and my hope for the
future be solely found in you. Let my wisdom for the
future come from you alone. "Know that wisdom is such
to your soul; if you find it, there will be a future, and your
hope will not be cut off." (Proverbs 24:14) My faith for my
future hope rests solely on you Lord. You will lead me
each step of the way- through this journey – and beyond it.
I am confident Lord that you have a plan, a plan "for
welfare and not for evil, to give me a future and a hope"
(Jeremiah 29:11) And that is what I rest in today Lord. The
plan and the promise that I can't see yet but resting in the
one who loves me more than life. "Now faith is the
assurance of things hoped for, the conviction of things not
seen." (Hebrews 11:1) Amen.

PRAYER NOTES

_____
_____
_____
_____
_____
_____
_____
_____
_____
_____
_____
_____
_____
_____
_____
_____
_____
_____
_____
_____
_____
_____
_____

Rebecca VanDeMark

ABOUT THE AUTHOR

Rebecca VanDeMark is a writer, speaker, and blogger who loves Jesus, life, and the miracle of hope. Rebecca is the founder of SEEN Gathering*, a chronic illness ministry and owns a handmade company, December Caravan, which donates a portion of all of its proceeds to charity. Rebecca holds degrees from Cedarville University and Regent University and a certificate from American University. Before fighting health issues Rebecca worked in Washington DC with two non-profit organizations and later taught High School History and Bible Classes for seven years. Rebecca loves celebrating the beauty of the ordinary each day as she fights Advanced Lyme Disease and Cancer in addition to other health issues. She lives with her family, splitting time between the sweet south and upstate New York. Rebecca can be found at her personal website (www.rebeccavandemark.com) or her blog (www.caravansonnet.com). She welcomes emails at: rebeccavandemark@gmail.com.

*To connect with SEEN Gathering please visit the website at: www.seengathering.org.

34499648R00047

Made in the USA
Middletown, DE
23 August 2016